W9-CLH-275

THE SHAKERS

J
289.
80973
William

012

THE SHAKERS

Jean Kinney Williams

American Religious Experience

Franklin Watts
A Division of Grolier Publishing
New York / London / Hong Kong / Sydney
Danbury, Connecticut

Interior design by Molly Heron
Photographs ©: Ann Chwatsky: cover, 8, 10, 12, 19, 41, 49, 52, 62, 72, 82,
96, 98, 99, 100; Corbis-Bettmann: 23, 33, 34, 36, 37, 43, 54, 67, 68, 86, 89;
North Wind Picture Archives: 30; Shaker Museum and Library, Old Chatham,
New York: 80, 91, 95; UPI/Corbis-Bettmann: 13, 28, 58, 61, 76.

Library of Congress Cataloging-in-Publication Data

Williams, Jean Kinney.
The Shakers / by Jean Kinney Williams.

p.   cm.—(American religious experience)
Includes bibliographical references and index.
Summary: Examines the history, beliefs, way of life, and current
status of this humble and devout Christian group.

ISBN 0-531-11342-6
1. Shakers—United States—History—Juvenile literature. [1. Shakers.]
I. Title. II. Series.
BX9766.W55   1996
289'.8'0973—dc21 96–51498
CIP
AC

© 1997 Jean Kinney Williams
All rights reserved. Published simultaneously in Canada
Printed in the United States of America
1 2 3 4 5 6 7 8 9 10 R 06 05 04 03 02 01 00 99 98 97

CONTENTS

THE SHAKERS

WHO ARE THE SHAKERS?

One of the most devout Christian groups in American history is today best remembered for their furniture and crafts, which sometimes sell for tens of thousands of dollars. But if it had not been for the Shakers' deep religious roots, those chairs and wooden boxes might not have been worth remembering.

The United Society of Believers in Christ's Second Appearing earned their nickname, the Shakers, because of the shaking and shivering convulsions that overcame them in worship in their early days in England and in the new country of the United States of America, where they sought freedom from religious persecution. Full of the spirit of God, they shook their sins away and sought perfection. Over the years, their sometimes wild movements gave way to orderly group dances and marches.

They believed Jesus Christ had made his second appearance as promised in the Bible not at the end of the world, but in the person of Ann Lee. She was an illiterate factory worker from Manchester,

England, who saw to it that the building of heaven on Earth was begun. Which brings us back to those simple but beautiful wooden chairs and boxes: anything being made for heaven has to be special, to say the least, if not perfect. "The peculiar grace of a Shaker chair is due to the fact that it was made by someone capable of believing that an angel might come and sit on it," said Thomas Merton, a

Brother Arnold Hadd, one of eight Shakers living in the remaining Shaker village in Sabbathday Lake, Maine, making a chair; in recent decades, the Shakers have become well known for their beautifully crafted furniture.

greatly admired Roman Catholic monk who was interested in the different ways of worshipping God.

But the Shakers actually are special for what they accomplished in their series of communities, an experiment in living that makes them unique in the history of Christianity. At one time they numbered in the thousands, their membership peaking in the decades just before the Civil War, with Shaker villages spread from Maine to western Indiana. Today there are eight Believers in the Society, still living in what was once considered the least of the eighteen villages, at Sabbathday Lake, Maine. There, two "brothers" and six "sisters" carry on the more than two-hundred-year-old Shaker traditions of celibacy (remaining unmarried), manual labor, and, in general, a simple life of receiving and sending out God's love. There are eight of them following the gospel of Ann Lee, just as there were eight who came to America with her in 1774.

Many of their villages have been turned into museum sites. Today, visitors can see what might have drawn the typical eighteenth- or nineteenth-century evangelistic Christian in search of salvation to the Shakers: freshly painted buildings with spotless windows, quiet building interiors rich with polished wooden floors and cupboards, villages laid out in the picturesque New England countryside or the lush Ohio Valley.

The Shakers promised more than an attractive home. Many converts spoke of the abundant love between members, who all had what was considered important work to do, whether it was spiritually guiding a "family," gathering in crops, or weaving cloth. A widow with young children often did not consider the requirement of celibacy to be such a bad thing when she knew her children would be well cared for in an extended Shaker "family." She could

Each Shaker "family" living within a Shaker village was supposed to be as self-sufficient as possible. That would have included, for example, making their own fabric for clothing, beginning with spinning, dying, and weaving wool sheared from their sheep.

contribute to this group and receive life's necessities from it according to her talents and needs.

Life in America slowly changed throughout the nineteenth century, however. Once the Civil War ended, the country that had almost split in half instead began to grow, as those looking for new economic opportunities headed west to the prairies and beyond. In

Sister Mildred Barker, who headed the Sabbathday Lake Shakers until her death in 1990, is holding a pin cushion that, along with the spinning wheel and other items, was to be auctioned off. As the Shaker population declined, more and more of their household and farm items were sold to help support the remaining members.

the east, the cities grew larger and the rural population began to shrink, and religious salvation became less urgent. The quiet country life of the Shakers called to fewer and fewer people, and it became increasingly difficult for the Society of Believers to hang on to those converts already won. The "world's people," as outsiders were referred to, once jammed the Believers' worship services to be entertained by the dancing and marching. But they quit coming, and the dancing stopped, because the Shaker population had grown too old to keep it up. The Believers, considering themselves a chosen people, seemed destined to sink into oblivion as one Shaker village after another closed.

It was well into the twentieth century that the "world's people" once again discovered the Shakers. They first discovered a Shaker legacy: their beautiful handiwork. Friends of the remaining Shakers as well as antiques dealers began buying up excess furniture and other items to be used in Shaker museum displays or in Shaker villages that were themselves turned into museums. Shaker pieces that made it to auction blocks were sold for exorbitant prices. Gradually, more and more people sought out what the few remaining Shakers had to say. Today, the small group at Sabbathday Lake includes converts still in their thirties as well as elderly lifelong members. They think Shakerism is here to stay.

ANN LEE, AN UNLIKELY LEADER

2

*I*n 1774, the American colonies of England were grumbling about being heavily taxed by, but not represented in, the English Parliament. The dawn of a new era for the western world was soon to come.

That summer, a band of English immigrants was on its way to America, totally uninterested in the political situation between England and America. This small group of men and women, dubbed the "Shaking Quakers" and led by a woman named Ann Lee, were members of a radical new church that was no longer welcome in England. A vision from God, she said, told her to take her small religious group to America.

Their worship services were unusual, with people twirling about, leaping into the air, trembling, falling and rolling around on the ground, or shaking and shouting, as they felt moved by the spirit of God. This behavior earned them the nickname "Shakers" and was enough to stir the mockery and anger of other Christians. But then the Shakers began to barge into other churches during their more conventional worship services, shouting to the congregations about the Shaker view of religious truth, and jail sentences for the Shakers became more common.

The Shakers got their start at the home of their first leaders, a couple named James and Jane Wardley, in Manchester, England. Manchester was an industrial town full of factories where men, women, and even children worked long days under rugged conditions. The Wardleys were tailors and had been members of the Quakers, a religious group formed about one hundred years earlier in England. But the Wardleys formed a sect with other Christians who agreed with the Quakers' pacifism—the belief that all war was wrong, no matter what the circumstances. Like the Quakers, this new sect caused controversy by rejecting the Christian notion of the Trinity, in which God is considered to be three beings: the Father, the Son (Jesus Christ), and the Holy Spirit. One woman who joined their group, Ann Lee, ended up as its leader.

At first she may not have seemed much like leadership material. She was the daughter of a blacksmith, and is thought to have been born on Leap Day (February 29) in 1736, in her parents' home on Toad Lane in Manchester. She and her many siblings spent much of their childhood working fourteen-hour days in the mills and factories of the city and were illiterate. Ann Lee married another blacksmith, Abraham Stanley, at her parents' insistence and against her own wishes. She never found any happiness with her husband and was heartbroken over the loss of all four of their children, three in infancy and one as a small child.

Ann's devoutness and boldness in proclaiming the Shakers' Christian beliefs gradually won her leadership of the small radical sect, which included her father and brother. The group's worship services at the Wardleys' home could be heard throughout the neighborhood, as they shouted, sang, and danced. Each person would act as they felt led by the spirit of God, and services ended only when all were exhausted. To outsiders, the services appeared chaotic. By the early 1770s, several members of the group had been arrested. In one case, they entered another local church and disrupted the pastor's sermon. Another time, group members were charged with destroying another church's property.

Shaker history says that it was while she was imprisoned that Ann Lee had a vision from God that the four children to whom she gave birth all died because she had committed the sin of having sexual relations with her husband. When the Wardleys told Ann that they, too, had stopped having marital relations, Ann felt she had found one element for a holier and more spiritual way of life: celibacy.

After that vision, Ann Lee "revealed herself as Ann the Word," or one through whom God would speak, much like Jesus of Nazareth, wrote Edward R. Horgan in his book *The Shaker Holy Land: A Community Portrait*.[1] After that, she became known as Mother Ann. In spite of her gender and low social status, she became the leader of the small group that by now called itself the Shakers. The group included some socially prominent men and eventually even some converted clergymen. She led the Shakers in England for four more years, until another vision from God promised success in America, where, they believed, they could establish a true church. She and eight others emigrated to America on a ship called *Mariah* in 1774.

Historians wish they knew more about Ann Lee and the early days of the Shakers. Probably because she was illiterate, the group generally placed little importance on written records. One legend, though, about Ann Lee that was popular with the Shakers is a story about their trip aboard *Mariah*. The ship's captain and crew, according to the legend, were tired of the Shakers' noisy worship services, which could erupt at any time, and they threatened to throw the whole group overboard.

In the meantime, a wooden plank on the ship came loose, causing a leak. Ann told the captain not to worry because two angels were guarding the ship. Just then a huge wave knocked into the ship, pushing the loose plank back into place. From then on, the captain allowed the nine Shakers to worship as they wished until they landed safely in New York City in August.

Because they arrived with few resources, the mission of spreading their faith would have to wait. The group split up to look for work, several of them heading for the area around Albany, New York. Ann Lee and her husband found work in New York, living with and working for a family. Another member of the group, John Hocknell, returned to England to get his family and return with money to buy land. Because of Ann's insistence on being celibate, her husband eventually left her.

When Hocknell got back to the United States in 1776, the Shakers gathered at the property he bought near Albany, at a place called Niskeyuna. Their main tasks were to clear the land, drain the swamp, grow food, and build dwellings.

Two revolutions were sweeping the colonies. One was political, with rebel colonists fighting the army of England and King George III to establish an independent country. Another revolution was spiritual, as many Americans sought more in their religious lives than was offered by New England's Congregational Church, the tradi-

Sister Mildred Barker working at a weaving loom; Mother Ann taught the Shakers to "put your hands to work and give your hearts to God," and any Shaker still capable of working had some kind of job to do.

tional New England church established by the Puritans. An era called the Great Awakening had begun in the 1740s, and many Protestants were searching for new ways to commune with God personally, leaving established churches behind.

The Shakers were hardly aware of the Revolutionary War going on in New England, as they toiled daily to establish a settlement. One of Mother Ann's most enduring sayings supposedly came from this time: she told her fellow Shakers, "Put your hands to work and give your heart to God." This advice would encourage a strong work ethic among Shakers for decades to come.

After each day's hard work, the group always found the energy to worship in their unusual way. They believed that the Millennium, or time of Christ's reappearance on Earth, had come. Millennialism, based on the Biblical books of Daniel and Revelation, promises a thousand-year reign of Christ on Earth. The Shakers believed that this time, the spirit of Christ had appeared in a woman: Ann Lee. She told them, however, that it was not yet time to spread their gospel. Other leaders of the group in addition to Mother Ann were her brother, William, and another Englishman, James Whittaker.

As the Revolutionary War heated up, religious fervor in the form of revivals spread throughout Massachusetts and New York, and the isolation of the Shakers ended. A revival meeting in nearby New Lebanon, New York, brought hundreds of religious seekers to the area, and word of the Shaker movement spread, bringing their small, struggling community a variety of visitors by about the year 1780. One of those visitors was a minister in the New Light Baptist movement, Joseph Meacham, who was received by Mother Ann with the warm hospitality she showed all visitors. Meacham became convinced he had found that for which he "had so earnestly prayed," as he later said; he and much of his congregation joined the community at Niskeyuna.[2]

What was it that early converts such as Meacham found appealing? The Congregational Church had very strict views about the relationship between God and people. They believed that some people in the world were destined *not* to be in Heaven with God after their death, no matter what. That concept, called predestination, bothered many Christians, and it inspired some to find a different way of interpreting the Bible and worshipping God. Also, the mainstream churches claimed that visions and messages from God were no longer possible and had ended with the era of the very early Christian church in the days of the Roman Empire; there were many Christians, though, who did not believe these messages had ended. In addition to the Shakers were several bands of Protestants who believed the Millennium was near, that Christ would soon return to Earth to separate the holy from the unholy.

Those who stumbled upon the Shakers in their humble cabins found a group who, like others of that day, believed revelations from God were still possible. Many pious Christians were drawn to the Shaker belief that by regularly confessing their sins to a group leader such as Mother Ann and giving up their marriage beds, the second coming of Christ would occur, in their hearts. Mother Ann believed celibacy was a key step for Shakers in creating this new world, which would be heaven on Earth. "You must forsake the marriage of the flesh or you cannot be married to the Lamb," or have Jesus Christ truly present in your heart, she is said to have told converts.[3] Celibacy usually was the most difficult part of Shaker life for converts to accept, but it made sense to many that love for all men, women, and children in general must be stronger than one's love for immediate family. Another important element of Shakerism was giving up one's private possessions and sharing them with all in the community, as practiced by the early Christian church.

Although there are no portraits of her, Ann Lee seems to have had an enchanting personality and "keen and penetrating" blue eyes, according to two of her followers who wrote about her later.[4] Her confidence in her teachings and her simple and sincere way of life were further reasons visitors often became converts, one of whom later recalled the joy and spirituality she exuded. Ann supposedly could read others' thoughts and would know about their lives before she was told anything by them. She prophesied about the sect's future and was credited with many healings. She and other Shakers gladly slept on the floors so that visitors could have a bed on which to sleep.

Husbands and wives with their children, and even large extended families, often joined the Shaker community, willing to accept men and women as well as people of all races as equals, strive for perfection in their work, give up their own possessions as they worked for the community, and dance as they worshipped God, who, they were taught, was Mother as well as Father. While known as Shakers, they gave their movement the official name of United Society of Believers in Christ's Second Appearing, often referring to themselves as Believers.

In the meantime, there was a war going on. Because they were English and refused to bear arms for the revolutionary cause, the Shakers were looked upon suspiciously. Mother Ann was charged with treason and jailed for six months in 1780. Her followers convinced local authorities that she was not an English sympathizer, and

Bedrooms were separate for men and women in each family house, and husbands and wives no longer lived with each other or their own children. This is a simply furnished bedroom in one "family" home in the Hancock, Massachusetts, Shaker village.

upon her release from jail she set out on a missionary journey. Not all converts had been able to move to Niskeyuna; some still were scattered throughout New England, and Ann, accompanied by her brother, William, and James Whittaker, wanted to visit them and encourage them in their new lives.

She was invited to Harvard, Massachusetts, to stay with followers of a religious leader named Shadrack Ireland. He had died a few years earlier, but his adherents still lived in his large house. Like Ann Lee, Ireland had preached living in community and pacifism, and many of his followers became disciples of Mother Ann. Ireland's property soon would become known as the Harvard Shaker village, and another community was established nearby at Shirley, Massachusetts. The number of converts, many living in either Niskeyuna or Harvard, was more than four hundred by February 1781.

As they traveled, though, the Shaker leaders provoked the wrath of other communities where they were strangers. After they arrived in Harvard, a meeting was called to "remove the people called Shaking Quakers" from the town, as a public notice announced.[5] James Whittaker met a crowd coming to evict them from the Ireland property. He convinced most of them that the Shakers were harmless, and they were able to remain there during the fall and winter of 1781.

But the town's suspicions of this new Society of Believers were not appeased for long. Shaker apostates (those who joined and then left the group) and visitors to the communities gave reports on the unusual worship services. One observer, who went on to become governor of New Hampshire and a U.S. senator, told of behavior "so wild and extravagant that it was some time before I could believe my own senses."[6] He described a woman who twirled about for almost an hour because, she said, to stop would be "blasphemy against God."[7]

Off and on during 1781 and 1782, the townspeople of Harvard would confront the Shaker leaders, who continued to stay there, and question them or try to intimidate them. The Revolutionary War had not ended yet, and people still wondered if the Shakers were pro-British. Many felt threatened by their ideas of property sharing, and celibacy often was seen as something that broke up families, especially when one spouse joined the Shakers and the other did not. Ann's brother William, for example, had left a wife and son to join the Shakers.

As the sect grew, so did the alarm of the local residents. Finally, after an especially boisterous meeting at the Ireland house that could be heard throughout the area, a mob from Harvard surrounded the house, dragged Ann Lee and other Shakers outside, and forced them to leave town. The mob accompanied them as they walked several miles to the town of Lancaster, beating and whipping them along the way, especially the English Shakers.

Ann and William Lee and James Whittaker did not return to Niskeyuna until autumn of 1783. They visited with scattered Shakers, staying where they were welcomed and often encountering other persecutors. William Lee and Whittaker suffered another brutal beating earlier that year, and when they returned to New York, Ann and William were exhausted. William died the next summer, and Ann told her followers she soon would be gone as well. Without any sign of illness, she grew weaker, then died on September 8, 1784, at the age of forty-eight. When her body was exhumed in 1835 to be moved to a new grave site, it was discovered that she had suffered a fractured skull, most likely from having been dragged feet first down a flight of stairs during a mob raid. She lived long enough to see her movement started and had prophesied that it would spread southwest of New England. But the true character of the Shakers was yet to be established.

ALL THINGS IN COMMON

*A*fter Mother Ann's death, a few converts left the community, disappointed to discover that she was not immortal, and a handful of English Shakers left when they were passed over for leadership. Those who stayed, under the authority of James Whittaker, Joseph Meacham, and another convert, Lucy Wright, would grow to become the true Shakers who intrigued America and even foreign tourists in future decades.

One challenge for Mother Ann's successors was the many memories of her, even though her era of leadership in America was brief, only four years. But it was a fairly smooth transition when Whittaker, one of Ann Lee's most loyal converts, assumed control of the Society of Believers at Niskeyuna in 1784. He had suffered with Ann and William on their missionary journeys and was a strong preacher. He had done most of the public speaking along the way, denouncing the ways of the world and warning of God's impending judgment.

"Father James," as he was called, was especially concerned with the importance of celibacy and claimed to be free of any sexual desire. While Mother Ann had realized that not everyone could live a celibate life, and thought that marrying and raising a family were the least sinful of wrongs, Whittaker took no middle ground on the issue. "I hate your fleshly lives," he told his own non-Shaker family

Larger Shaker buildings, such as the dwellings and meetinghouses, had separate doors for men and women. That was one way to help prevent men and women from having any physical contact with each other.

members in a letter. He referred to his parents as "a stink in my nostrils" because they would not live a Shaker life.[1] Though he was not as harsh toward the Shakers themselves, he expected all Shakers to sever their family ties, as he had.

Whittaker realized the importance of more structure among the Shakers; he demanded obedience from the converts, whereas Mother Ann appears to have been a somewhat flexible leader with her diverse group of converts. He moved the center of leadership to New Lebanon, New York, and visited the scattered converts, looking for good leaders and encouraging them in their efforts to pool their resources and build strong communities away from "the world."

New communities were established in Maine and New Hampshire, and the first Shaker meetinghouse for worship was raised at New Lebanon in 1785. There, Father James established the practice of having separate doors in dwellings and meetinghouses for men and women. "Men and women shall not intermix in this house or yard, nor sit together," Whittaker admonished the Shakers in their new church.[2] Inside the larger Shaker buildings were separate stairways, and outdoor paths were made in pairs, so that men and women would have fewer chances to come into physical contact. Even in death, when buried in cemeteries, the Shakers remained separate by gender.

Father James' years of leadership, like Mother Ann's, were brief. He died at Enfield, Connecticut, in 1787, at the age of thirty-six, the last of the English immigrants who came to America with Ann Lee. At his death, he was more generous toward non-Shakers, as well as current Shakers, by leaving money for "the Poor the Widdows and the fatherless."[3] Within a few months, the American convert, forty-five-year-old Joseph Meacham, became head of the Shakers. He was

readily accepted—Mother Ann had predicted he would lead the group someday and had called him "the wisest man that has been born of woman for six hundred years."[4] His organizational skills turned the early Shaker villages into the orderly communes that would fascinate others in later years.

One of Meacham's first acts was to choose a woman, Lucy Wright, to lead the female Shakers throughout the Society, which he thought was in accordance with Mother Ann's plans and beliefs. Wright, born in 1760, was from a prominent Rhode Island family and had married into the Goodrich family, many of whom became Shakers. She had no children, had kept her maiden name, and was a prized convert of Mother Ann, who told the other Shaker sisters at Niskeyuna to look up to Lucy as their model. She and Meacham were called Mother Lucy and Father Joseph, and they also made their headquarters at New Lebanon. By now, the Niskeyuna Shaker settlement, where Mother Ann is buried, was known as Watervliet. Though it ceased to be the seat of Shaker government, its residents enjoyed the prestige of living in the original village.

In 1787, the Shakers were living in settlements that still were only loosely structured. Meacham is credited with gathering most of the remaining, scattered Shakers throughout New England into

There were thousands of Shakers in their peak membership years, as reflected in this large family dwelling built in 1837 in the Shaker village at Enfield, Connecticut.

communities that had established leaders and routines. Evangelization slowed down as internal organization became the focus.

In addition to the new meetinghouse at New Lebanon, the Shakers at first used buildings donated by converts, then began building new ones, such as the "Great House," which was a dwelling house, and various work buildings, such as spinning or bake houses. The other villages followed suit, and the architecture was kept simple. For example, meetinghouses were to have no spires, as Mother Ann did not like the look of "devil's steeple houses" that traditional churches used.[5]

Meacham structured each village to have three "families" with their own dwelling houses and barns, and each with their own leaders. Elders and eldresses were spiritual leaders of each family, deacons and deaconesses oversaw the farming and other work operations, and male trustees took care of financial matters with outsiders. (Women did not serve as trustees until the late 1800s.) Father Joseph and Mother Lucy chose men and women from among the best converts at New Lebanon to lead families in the other villages.

By the 1790s, just ten years after Mother Ann's death, there were nine Shaker villages, including the only one still in existence today, at Sabbathday Lake, Maine. By the year 1800, each village had approximately one hundred members. The hostile attitude of the townspeople at Harvard and Shirley subsided as they accepted their Shaker neighbors and even admired their tidy farms and villages. Most Shaker village residents were adult converts of working age; by the late eighteenth century, there still were few children among them.

Trying to be like the early Christians, who "had all things in

This is a drawing of the Shaker village at Canterbury, New Hampshire, which closed only in 1992.

common," as it states in the Bible's Acts of the Apostles, Shaker converts would pay off their debts and bring their household goods and animals to the communities. (Dogs, though, were not allowed, as Mother Ann had thought they housed evil spirits, and in general they were seen as pets that would only distract children from necessary work, prayers, or affection for people.) Wealthier converts often contributed land for the new settlement, as well as buildings. The typical converts, however, had fewer belongings to contribute: one couple who joined Watervliet in the 1790s brought with them 13 English pounds (a small amount of money), some furniture, a couple of yards of lace, a few pins, some shoe leather, and half of a pound of tea.[6]

Shakers kept rooms tidy by hanging up almost everything, sometimes even chairs, on pegs. That made it easier to sweep and clean floors.

Once in the communities, husbands and wives separated. Their children lived in quarters for boys or girls rather than with their parents, as they were now considered part of their larger Shaker family. Under Father Joseph, Shaker life became fairly regimented throughout the villages: they all knew when to get up, when to rest, when to eat, and when to have meetings. Six hours was allotted for each night's sleep. Rules were unwritten but understood: all sins were to be confessed, and awareness of others' sins observed, before each Sunday meeting, and there was to be no unnecessary talking or touching between males and females. Those who had tried Shaker life for a period and were ready to commit themselves to it signed a covenant. Meacham implemented this mainly to protect the Shakers from apostates (those who joined and then left), who often wanted back pay for their community work.

Meacham also is thought to have been the author of the pamphlet *A Concise Statement of the Only True Church* (there were few Shakers who would have been capable of writing it) in the 1790s. It explained Shaker doctrine to the public, but without any mention of Ann Lee. Perhaps Meacham was being cautious not to alarm potential converts who would not accept a woman as a savior from God. Meacham eliminated the sometimes wild expressions of spirituality from the worship services and replaced them with standardized dance steps, such as the "Square Order Shuffle," a marching dance that enthralled community visitors for the next several decades. Mother Lucy taught the sisters and brothers to dance with their hands cupped, palms up, as a way of receiving the Holy Spirit. Meacham also added "union meetings" to Shaker life, where a few pairs of men and women met several times each week to discuss various topics and develop helpful friendships. The women could mend

35

Monroe County Library System
Monroe, Michigan 48161

Dance was an important part of Shaker worship services from the time the sect formed until after the Civil War. "The world's people," such as the woman wearing a large hat in the lower left corner of this picture, often visited the services to watch, considering it great entertainment.

clothing for the men, for example, and the men could help the women with heavier chores.

Meacham's goal was to structure all aspects of Shaker life, from their finances, to their work, to how they interacted with each other, and even to the amount of sleep they got, with the hope of eliminating individual competition among them. By assigning all financial matters to male and female trustees within each family, Meacham made sure only a few people dealt with outsiders and handled money, considered to be too much of a reminder of the world and its temptations. Living in community had really just begun in earnest when Father Joseph assumed leadership of the Society of Believers. When he died in 1796, there were hundreds of converts living communal lives. Leadership of the entire sect fell to Mother Lucy, who benefited from the work ethic instituted by Mother Ann, the strict obedience to Shaker teachings demanded of converts by Father James, and the community structure put into place by Father Joseph. Under Lucy Wright, the Shakers would take yet another step forward.

CONVERTS TO THE SHAKER FAITH

4

Shortly before he died, Meacham is believed to have told Mother Lucy that "your Mother will have the gifts of God for you after I am gone," referring to Ann Lee.[1] There were Shakers who did not easily accept Lucy Wright's leadership, because she was a woman, but eventually most did. She proved to be skilled at organization, and she appointed able and loyal assistants. The twenty-five years in which she presided over the Society of Believers were years of growth and prosperity for the sect.

Wright continued on Meacham's path of tightening the organization of each village, and she also increased efforts at gathering in new converts. Many Americans were searching for a Christian way of life that looked to the next world, or the spiritual world of God, and turned away from the world of man. Wright established a "gathering order" in each village, or grouped newer converts together so that they could receive more attention and instruction in Shaker gospel. One important new member was a schoolteacher, Seth

Youngs Wells, who visited his Shaker uncle at New Lebanon and converted in 1799. He brought along his parents and nine siblings, all of whom remained faithful Shakers. Another was Issachar Bates, a Baptist minister who converted in 1805 after a two-year visit to Watervliet. A Revolutionary War veteran with eleven children, Bates became an effective missionary; one Vermont town to which he took the Shaker gospel saw twenty-five of its citizens join various communities of Believers.

Not all converts could move to the villages. Some remained at their homes with non-Shaker family members. And while in general the Shakers lived in peace with their neighbors, many still saw them as a threatening force that broke apart families.

Thomas Brown was a New York convert who eventually left the Watervliet Shakers, tiring of the exact obedience required of the rank-and-file members. He wrote a book about his years with the sect, in which he describes an experience he had as a missionary: the husband in an Albany, New York, family had expressed interest in Shakerism, and Brown visited him at his home. He found the man's wife "all in a rage; she ordered me out of the house, got the horse whip, shook it over my head, round and about me with many threats," as the husband sat silent. Soon an older son returned home and "threatened to shoot me, or some way take my life."[2] Over the next several decades, the Shakers would fight many legal battles with people whose spouses joined and took their children with them.

But overall, the Shakers enjoyed a better reputation among other Christians than they had in their very early days. Gone were the worship services with shrieking and screeching and wild dancing, replaced with hymn singing and orderly dance routines. As taught by Mother Ann, their large dwellings, painted white, and

These bark baskets are among the simple but beautiful Shaker creations that are today considered very valuable as antiques.

villages were extremely neat and clean. They became known for their hard work and honesty, as their trade with outsiders began to increase. The earliest Shakers had done the difficult work of clearing land and establishing villages. Converts who came to a Shaker village in the early 1800s were more likely to see a well-organized group of men and women who lived fairly comfortably. One convert, David Rowley, a cabinetmaker from Connecticut, expressed his happiness with his new life: "I have never seen one moment since I set out in this blessed way but that I felt thankful for it." He said he would "recommend it to all souls who are sick of the vain world."[3]

The most important decision Mother Lucy made in her leadership of the Shakers was to send missionaries to the western frontier, which early in the 1800s included Ohio and Kentucky. The religious revivalism that had spread feverishly throughout the Northeast had reached the new settlements along the Ohio River Valley. Mother Ann had once foreseen bringing the Shaker gospel to this region, which she called the "southwest." The Presbyterian church was trying to bring organized religion to the Ohio valley region, and Mother Lucy decided the Society of Believers might find success there, too.

On the first day of the year 1805, three of the Shakers' most effective evangelists, Issachar Bates, the scholarly Benjamin Seth Youngs, and John Meacham, son of Father Joseph, set out from New York. They were indeed headed southwest, as Mother Ann had predicted. They put their belongings on one horse, and for two months traveled on foot over 1,200 miles (1,930 km) of wilderness trails.

The first western converts were a couple, the Worleys, who lived in a log cabin in Turtle Creek, Ohio, and whose property became the first Shaker property in the area. A large dwelling house was planned, but for a while, six Shakers lived with nine Worleys in their 18- by 20-foot (5.5- by 6-m) home. Several Shaker sisters arrived in the spring of 1806 to help start a settlement, and their home was a leaky log cabin. The new group cleared land for planting and cut and prepared wood for buildings. "We have not had one day of rest since we left you," one of the sisters wrote to friends back east, describing a life of continuous chores.[4] Like the New York Shakers of the 1780s, the western Shakers experienced the grueling hard work of building a community from scratch.

But their work was fruitful. Many New Light Presbyterians were attracted to the Shaker gospel, including a minister, Richard

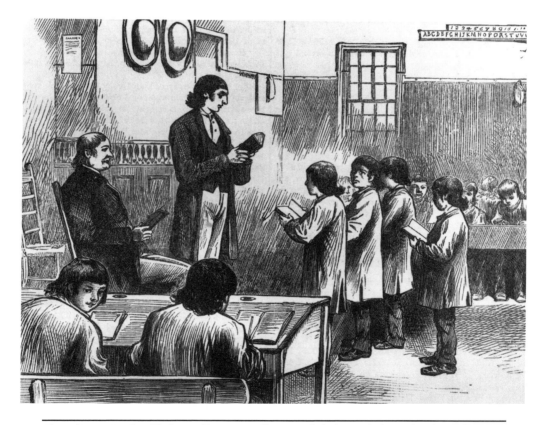

Boys living in the Shaker villages usually attended their Shaker schools in the winter months, when there wasn't any farm work to do. Girls attended in the summer.

SHAKER BUSINESSES

For the earliest Shakers in Niskeyuna, New York, life was a constant battle with the wilderness—land to be cleared, homes to be built, food to be grown. But "Mother" Ann Lee, endowed with an ability to inspire in her converts a passion for Shaker doctrine, also instilled in them a strong work ethic. The leaders who followed her, James Whittaker, Joseph Meacham, and Lucy Wright, managed to emphasize the importance of cooperative living. For example, most women in those days spun yarn for family clothing, among many other chores; but a typical Shaker woman, if it was her job for the time being, would spin for hours each day. Those conditions seemed to offer just the right background for a creative atmosphere in which Shakers came up with all sorts of inventions and marketing ideas.

In 1790, the Shakers were the first to package and market garden seeds, the high quality of which was well known, and Shaker herbs were shipped all over the country. A

McNemar, who brought much of his congregation with him to the Society of Believers. By 1812, the Turtle Creek settlement was known as Union Village, and its residents had erected two dwellings, a meetinghouse, and several work buildings in six years. By 1815, there were five western settlements: two each in Ohio and Kentucky and one in western Indiana. The two leading villages were Union

Philadelphia merchant advertised his Shaker products for sale, which included baskets, brooms, rocking chairs, diapers, and, of course, seeds.

Other Shaker gadgets that caught on across America were the springed clothespin, apple corers and peelers, metal pen points, and, perhaps their most famous invention, a clothes washing machine. Shaker women who had to bake large quantities of pies rigged their ovens with revolving baking trays to brown the pies evenly, and it was a Shaker woman, sitting at her spinning wheel one day, who came up with the idea for a circular saw. At first they didn't patent their inventions, believing them to be gifts from God that should be shared with all. But by 1828, they decided to patent some products, to ensure future income for the villages. As the number of children throughout the Society of Believers increased, so did the need for additional income. And some of the villages became almost wealthy; the Church Family at Hancock, Massachusetts, made $8,500 just from seeds one year in the 1830s.

Village in Ohio and Pleasant Hill in Kentucky; at Pleasant Hill, 128 converts signed the Shaker covenant in 1814.

The western Indiana village experienced almost constant struggle. Benjamin Seth Youngs was there and wrote home to New England about an apple orchard they had planted, though it would be awhile before it would produce any fruit. "I could easily drink three egg cups full of good cider this minute if I only had it. . . . I am already so tired and sick of this limy water."[5] In spite of those challenges, Youngs wrote an explanation of the Shaker gospel, *Testimony of Christ's Second Appearing*, that was circulated widely. It affected readers as far away as Ontario, Canada, where a woman, her husband, and their eight children converted. Another reader of Youngs' book, in New York City, decided he, too, was tired of the world's foolishness. He converted, along with a friend, six siblings, a brother-in-law, and four nieces and nephews. As a result of the evangelization during Mother Lucy's leadership, Shaker community populations increased by more than 40 percent. Their growth put a strain on leadership: many of the new Shaker village members were children of converts, and many of the adult converts were "winter Shakers," drawn more to the guarantees of meals and shelter than the Shaker gospel, and likely to move on in the spring.

There were always problems with apostates, from as early as Mother Ann's days. Valentine Rathbun was a Baptist minister who converted early in the 1780s. He was from nearby Pittsfield, Massachusetts, and convinced most of his congregation there to join the Shakers, too. One of those families included the Goodriches, whose twenty-four members included the future eldress Lucy Wright. Rathbun became angry with the Shakers when he was passed over for a leadership position, and he left within a few months.

Rathbun remained bitter, having "lost" much of his own family to the Shakers, and he wrote what would be the first of many Shaker "exposes." Shaker historian Stephen Stein notes that the exposes by former Shakers have proven to be a valuable source of information about the earliest Shakers, who apparently had little desire to record their history themselves. Apostates wrote about some of the more extreme behavior among the first Shakers, such as drunkenness and even running naked through the forests. Such anecdotes make it easier to understand the sometimes hostile attitudes toward them.

In the western communities, some ministers lost their congregations to the Shakers, and new converts were spurning (having no contact with) their families in "the world." The *Western Star* newspaper in Lebanon, Ohio, near Union Village, kept up a constant tirade of objections against the Shakers. An element of lawlessness on the frontier sometimes made life difficult for the fledgling Shaker communities. In Indiana, Issachar Bates wrote about a visit from a mob in 1808: "They came upon us on horseback with ropes to bind us." One mob leader told them, "Come prepare yourselves to move . . . for you have ruined a fine neighborhood, and now we intend to fix you."[6] But as time passed, the Indiana and other western Shakers, like their eastern Shaker brothers and sisters, came to be seen as able farmers and good neighbors.

The woman who gave the Shakers perhaps the most trouble was Mary Dyer from New England. She and her husband had converted and brought their children with them. When Mary decided not to stay with the Shakers, she wanted to take her children with her, while her husband wanted them to remain with the Shakers. She did leave with two of their children, but three remained. She spent the remainder of her years publicizing the accounts of her legal struggles with the Believers, and she wrote a 450-page book about the Society that used testimonies of other apostates to put the Shakers in the worst light possible. She never regained custody of the rest of her children.

Apostatizing was more common among male Shakers. In 1800,

in the New Lebanon Church Family (with some of the most committed Shakers), more than three-fourths of the males were age twenty-five to forty. These were the people who did much of the farm labor. By 1825, only 17 percent of the males were in that important age group. The women in that age group went from more than 60 percent to less than 30 percent. As more men and women left, it became more difficult for Mother Lucy and her successors to find capable leaders among those who remained.

Still, under Mother Lucy the Shakers continued to gather converts even as others left. As the communities grew, she saw the need to regularize their behavior more, warning them to "wake up to God" and quit their "vain jesting, joking, obscene and filthy communication," which seemed to be more commonplace between brothers and sisters.[7] She oversaw the establishment of schools in each village. By the mid-1800s, they would be among the best in the areas where Shakers lived and had many non-Shaker students. Mother Lucy wanted Shaker adults as well as children to improve their grammar, substituting "it will do" for "'twill does," for example.[8] But they still said "yea" and "nay" for yes and no.

It was Wright who allowed the Shakers to introduce hymns into their worship services, along with additional dances. She also standardized Shaker clothing for men and women; the men finally abandoned their eighteenth-century knee britches for trousers. The clothing was not fashionable but was designed for working and to hide men's and women's physiques.

Just before Mother Lucy died early in 1821, Brother Freegift Wells of Watervliet put into writing all the Shaker rules that could be recalled. He arranged them by subject, such as Sabbath worship,

*Four of the sisters and one brother working in the kitchen
in Sabbathday Lake*

separation of the sexes, and overall behavior. Mother Lucy rejected the project, still preferring to rely on oral tradition. This way, future Shaker leaders would not feel restricted to rules of the past. She also did not want those in "the world" to read the Shaker rules, fearing they would misunderstand them or see them out of context. She died in February 1821, leaving the Society of Believers after twenty-five years of growth (which included seven new influential communities in the west) and steady leadership. Shaker writer and historian Calvin Green sent the news to the other villages by writing, "many tears were shed . . . our Ever Blessed Mother is no more!"[9]

LIVING IN COMMUNITY

5

Though Lucy Wright wanted to continue to lead the Shakers with verbal instructions only, the Society had grown and spread out around the country to where that didn't seem possible anymore. So Freegift Wells' book, the *Millennial Laws,* was printed in 1821, after Mother Lucy's death. It addressed all aspects of Shaker life, from dealing with other people without becoming angry to how much interaction with outsiders was acceptable. It even included such details as how to properly clasp one's hands together. The village leaders welcomed the *Millennial Laws* as they attempted to mold the ever-larger number of Shaker converts into a cooperative group.

Alcohol drinking must have been somewhat of a problem among many Shakers, for *Millennial Laws* addressed that, too: no drinking on the Sabbath, unless doing hard work, and then only in the morning, but not before breakfast. Shaker historian Priscilla Brewer noted in her book *Shaker Communities, Shaker Lives* that in

Sabbathday Lake community members at morning prayer

1817 the New Lebanon Church Family bought seventy-one gallons of rum, plus several dozen gallons of other alcoholic drinks, in addition to what they would have made themselves.

By the 1820s, the Shakers were an established part of American life, and for more than twenty years they were under the direction of two lead eldresses and two lead elders. Their number at the time of Mother Lucy's death was not large for an entire church denomination: about four thousand community residents, including children. But considering what it was they were trying to do—live a celibate life apart from the world in self-sufficient communities, separated from non-Shaker family and friends, and without personal possessions—they were very successful. Their religion was a strong part of their everyday life, probably the main reason they were so successful at community life.

There have been other Americans who have tried living "in community." For example, author Nathaniel Hawthorne (he wrote *The Scarlet Letter* and *The House of the Seven Gables,* among other works) and other intellectuals tried communal living on Brook Farm, near Boston, Massachusetts. Their idea was to establish work roles for all inhabitants based on a law of "universal harmony." The farm project lasted until 1847, and Hawthorne later wrote about his experience there in satirical works. He also wrote about the Shakers, and though he admired their hard work and comfortable lives, he considered their worship services absurd.

As a girl in the 1840s, Louisa May Alcott, author of *Little Women,* and her sisters and parents were among a group who started up Fruitlands, a vegetarian community near Harvard, Massachusetts. Not only were animals not eaten, but they weren't used for farm labor; Bronson Alcott considered that unfair slave labor, and any animal product, such as cheese, milk, butter, or eggs, was off limits. Fruitlands was a neighbor of the Harvard Shaker group, but it did not last long. Most Fruitlands residents were more interested in philosophy than farming, and within a few years its members had gone on to other things.

Daily life for Shakers had settled into fairly consistent routines by the 1820s, and their villages and worship services even became

This circle dance performed during a Sunday service at New Lebanon, New York, shows how elaborate the choreography (or dance steps) became.

tourist attractions. Though their Sunday church–meeting dances were now choreographed, the Shakers still danced vigorously to symbolize the shaking off of sin. Visitors flocked to Shaker church services (often to ridicule them), and there were even separate doors for "the world's people" to enter the meetinghouses. The Shakers had begun to sing their own hymns; one, called "Son and Daughter," is about Jesus and Ann Lee:

> *The Father and the Spirit*
> *Have sent the blessed Two*
> *To visit the creation*
> *and teach us what to do.*

Another hymn about Ann Lee called her "ever blessed Mother," whom "Forever I'll adore."[1] Marching as a form of dance was introduced in the 1820s, enabling older Shakers to participate. And reacting loudly to God's spirit had not completely vanished: Union Village Shakers were known to stamp their feet so loudly during worship services that they could drown out the sound of thunder. Though often called fanatics, they believed themselves to be a chosen people, destined to become greater still.

Obedience was still a key to holding the Shakers together. Leaders, such as village elders and eldresses, were not interested in democracy, or the principle of majority rule. The democratic form of government in the United States, they believed, was actually harmful to mankind, because it led people to seek and put into action their own will rather than that of God; therefore, the Shakers were not voters. Because obedience was so important, so was the quality of leadership, and the Shakers were most likely to respect those leaders who themselves were once obedient rank-and-file members. Elders and eldresses and the deacons still had to conform to the rules of the lead ministry in New Lebanon, too. After all, Mother Lucy had reminded them, "True Believers are able to see the necessity of Order."[2] As spread apart as they were, and as big as their Society grew, it is remarkable that there were never any splits within the Shaker church (until the 1960s, when there were only a few members left). Those who came to find Shaker rules intolerable simply left it.

It was not uncommon for Shakers to leave the communities in order to marry each other. At the Pleasant Hill Shaker village in Kentucky, Believers considered it quite a blow to morale and their own struggle to remain celibate when two much-respected leaders, Elder James Gass and his wife, Lucy, left the community to resume their former married life. There were many instances recorded in family journals of one or another Shaker leaving, followed by news of his or her marriage.

But what of those who stayed? What was their everyday life like? It did vary somewhat from region to region, and it could also depend on the quality of local village leaders. For example, the apostate Thomas Brown just happened to fall under the leadership of the overzealous and sin-obsessed elder John Scott. Scott kept Brown prisoner in a shed while Brown decided whether he wanted to stay with the sect; such treatment made that decision easy for Brown. But another apostate who had grown up with the Shakers, Hervey Elkins, wrote of the good example set for all members by the elders and eldresses he encountered. In general, all Shakers had much in common with their brothers and sisters, from east to west. Camaraderie and close friendships between members of a Shaker family replaced relationships between spouses or immediate family members.

Most of the adult converts were evangelical Christians, and the most committed of the Shakers truly sought to serve God, first and foremost. One widow who, with her two young children, joined the community at New Lebanon wrote to a friend and described "such

Though one-time Shaker Hervey Elkins had much respect for Shaker elders and eldresses in general, one incident finally soured him on Shaker life in the early nineteenth century: he had observed, during the regular union meetings, that a Brother Urbino and a Sister Ellina had obvious feelings for each other. Another sister, jealous over the attention that Urbino and Ellina gave one another, made Ellina's life miserable. Ellina was moved to another community, and her death shortly after that, Elkins assumed, was from a broken heart. Though love and cooperation were the ideal for which Shakers were to strive, not all negative behavior could be stamped out.

Many Shakers ran off and married, often to the disgust of remaining community members. But one love story among them with a happier ending occurred later in the nineteenth century. Frank Stanton and Frankie Hobbs were two boys being raised by the Shakers at Harvard, and through their friendship they became more like brothers. Frankie had a sister, Edith, who didn't live there but visited often, and she also became good friends with Frank. Frankie died tragically young, in his teens, but his sister and Frank married a few years later, with the blessings of, and many gifts from, the Harvard Shaker community.

peace, such harmony and love I never saw before."[3] In families of between thirty and one hundred people, most lived together peacefully and learned to share material goods. While many Shakers were serious about forsaking the world's pleasures, some seemed more thankful for physical security than spiritual salvation. One Tyringham village brother was quoted in a 1849 magazine article as saying, "I am perfectly content. I have enough to eat and drink . . . good clothes to wear, a warm bed to sleep in, and just as much work as I like and no more."[4]

Hard work was a part of everyone's life, from children to the oldest members. Even women who were elderly and blind could knit stockings, while older men might do less physical work such as tailoring. Each family tried to be self-sufficient, with its own seamstresses and tailors, weavers, physicians, gardeners, etc. Jobs were often rotated to avoid "burnout" and tedium. One elder, Henry Blinn, who joined the Canterbury, New Hampshire, Shakers as a teenager in 1824, was famous among the Society for his skills as a beekeeper, author, teacher, dentist, blacksmith, and woodworker, in addition to his job as spiritual leader. Their hard work and striving for perfection in all they did was an expression of what they considered to be their religious duty. That work ethic also came to provide the Shaker villages with healthy incomes as their products, such as garden seeds, brooms, and furniture, were much sought after.

Eldress Gertrude Soule doing needlework in a 1978 photograph taken at the Canterbury village; at the time, she was one of three sisters remaining there.

Like most American children of that era, Shaker boys and girls had much work to do, too. Boys went to school in the winter months so that they could help with farm chores during the rest of the year. Girls attended school in the summer and helped adult women with domestic chores the rest of the year, such as spinning or cleaning or kitchen work. Cleaning was especially important to the Shakers, having been taught by Ann Lee that a good spirit will not live in a dirty house, and the girls learned to hang chairs up on wall pegs when they swept to get the floor even cleaner. All children had regular jobs in addition to schooling and seasonal work. Some typical chores for children included cutting bags for the seeds that Shakers were so successful in selling outside their communities, chopping firewood, and cutting ice.

Schools for children became part of every Shaker village, at first aiming only to teach trades and crafts to boys and domestic arts to girls. But by 1811, there were more than one hundred children enrolled in school at Union Village in Ohio, learning reading, spelling, and even manners, and the eastern schools introduced more academics into their schools as well. Seth Youngs Wells, who had been a schoolteacher before he converted, was put in charge of Shaker education.

The Shakers believed that love and positive role modeling were the most important parts of rearing future Shakers. At New Lebanon, teenager Elisha Blakeman was woodworking apprentice to Brother Luther Copley, who died in 1851. Young Blakeman wrote a poem about Copley, calling him his mentor as well as "A holy, honest, upright man/ A child of God and Mother Ann."[5] For many Shakers, though, being a children's caretaker was an unpleasant chore. When he was older and had moved from that job, poet Blakeman

Another Canterbury eldress, Bertha Lindsay, was photographed in 1978 in the one-room schoolhouse where she received her education as a girl in the Shaker village.

Three Sabbathday Lake Shakers sharing some gardening duties

wrote: "I'm now released from the boys/ And from a deal of din and noise."[6] Perhaps it's no wonder that not too many boys grew into adult Shakers! But recreation was a part of every Shaker's life, too, and children were taken on picnics, candy-buying excursions, and fishing trips, which adults enjoyed, too, especially in summer.

By the 1820s, as the number of young men among the Shakers continued to dwindle, it became increasingly necessary to hire out-side help for farm work, and the remaining Shaker men had more and more work to do, whatever their age. Temporal concerns, such as the amount of work to do and other matters of living conditions, began to push spiritual matters aside for some members. Eager for new members, some villages allowed "converts" who actually had very little devotion to Shakerism to join. These new arrivals often left within months and then perhaps came and went several more times. Though Shaker membership figures continued to grow, many of those counted were children who would eventually leave and other adults who did not necessarily remain as long-term members.

The Shakers had gotten the attention of mainstream Christians with their radical ideas of God and approach to life. Now they themselves, busier than ever with "worldly" concerns such as finances and work, would undergo a shaking up, a reawakening to what they considered to be God's gifts and which they called "Mother's Work."

MOTHER'S WORK

6

*A*s the Shakers' numbers grew, their temporal concerns did,
too. Family dwellings were busy from sunup to sundown,
as members tried to keep their various families of
Believers self-sufficient and as the market for their products
increased. Disasters, such as flooding or fires, could ravage a village's or family's finances. Sometimes a trustee, the only family
member who watched over money, made bad investments or even
ran off with cash. When other members would leave, they usually
received a gift from the community, in cash and/or goods, to get
them started in their life in "the world." Many Shakers simply
found the regimented life too stifling, and their leaving often
would be noted in family journals with critical comments. One
elder who left after twenty years with the Shakers was referred to
as "a most filthy creature" in the journal entry that noted his
leaving.[1] And as apostasy increased, so did the work pressure
among those who remained. All Shaker communities, from the

two-family group in Whitewater, Ohio, to the seven families in New Lebanon, shared in these same problems.

Because there were still enough members, however, to make the kinds of sacrifices demanded by the sect's doctrine, the Shakers actually flourished in America during the period between Mother Lucy's death in 1821 and the Civil War. By mid-century, the population of Shaker villages totaled six thousand (though not all had signed covenants). Like the rest of America, the Shakers were quite interested in technological advances. Though the Shakers didn't have much use for democracy or American politics, they gained much from the country's capitalist economy. They put their socialistic lifestyle to work, designing and manufacturing products such as clothespins and brooms, and sold them to eager customers. Shaker trustees, who until about the year 1900 were exclusively male, often became traveling salesmen, peddling Shaker products as they traveled throughout big- and small-town America. By the 1830s, the Shakers were making "fancy" items that they did not use themselves, such as silk-trimmed baskets. In some respects, their own tastes grew more worldly as well. It was getting more difficult to keep younger members and convince them of the value of the Shaker doctrine.

The Shakers became quite an object of curiosity among "the world," and books and articles by apostates about the Shakers were as marketable as Shaker household products. Writers and others frequently visited the communities, usually more impressed with their living conditions, such as the lush fields and tidy villages, than with their ideas on religion. One of their most famous visitors was Charles Dickens; he wrote about his impressions in his book *American Notes,* and the word he used most often to describe Shaker life was "grim": "We walked into a grim room, where several grim hats were hanging on grim pegs. . . . Ranged against the wall were six or eight stiff high-backed chairs [which] partook so strongly of the general grimness" that one would have no desire to sit on them.[2]

One facet, or key point, of the Shaker faith was the belief that visions or messages from God were always possible. In the 1830s, a phenomenon swept through the Shakers, who, though they may still

The unusual round stone barn in the Hancock, Connecticut, village is one of the most famous Shaker landmarks.

This group photograph taken at New Lebanon illustrates how women began to greatly outnumber men among the Shakers, a trend that became a problem in the nineteenth century. Younger men, who did most of the farm work, became less and less likely to join or stay with the Shakers as the century wore on.

have looked "grim" to outsiders, were reveling in what they considered to be quite a variety of spiritual gifts from God and Mother Ann. This spiritual influence helped spark interest among younger members in the traditional Shaker values and doctrine. It happened at a time when the Shakers were preoccupied with materialistic matters, and was an era that lasted for more than ten years. It came to be known as "Mother's Work," a time the Shakers later compared to the first century of Christianity, which also was known for many spiritual phenomena.

"Mother's Work" began in August 1837, at Watervliet, New York. Several teenage sisters in a classroom suddenly stopped what they were doing and began first to tremble, then whirl around, not stopping until they fainted. Upon awakening, they told of a journey to heaven and brought greetings from angels in the next world. Other children in Watervliet, and then adults, began having similar experiences. In some ways, it was not unusual. Shakers in Ohio and Kentucky had always reported much in the way of visions and spiritual dreams, as well as healings, and occasionally Shakers everywhere would tell of visits or encounters with their late leaders or other spiritual figures, all of which were taken seriously. But "Mother's Work" permeated the entire society and became the main focus of the Shakers' lives for several years after 1837.

The intensity of the phenomena of that era sounds exhausting: early on, at Watervliet, children would spend hours shaking or writhing, often until midnight. Other Shaker villages (there were eighteen of them at the time) heard of it, and the spiritual activity spread. The public heard about it, too, and packed the meetinghouses on Sundays to watch.

Much of the activity was focused on "instruments," or people who claimed to be mediums through whom various spiritual figures spoke. There was also a lot of spiritual "travel" going on; one young sister spent six days in a trance. A typical "instrument" was Ann Mariah Goff, a fourteen-year-old resident of Watervliet who had elaborate visions. Some of them lasted several hours and consisted of visits with Mother Ann, who had advice for the Shakers, such as to repent and become more humble. Mother Ann, they believed, was telling them to purge any worldly influences that had crept into the Shakers' lives; their prayers and even their housecleaning intensified. As the goings-on became more unusual and unpredictable, the Shakers closed their worship meetings to the public, fearing that they would appear shocking.

Meanwhile, some of the most famous names in history were paying the Shakers visits, according to instruments: Shakers claimed to have "seen" Noah, Alexander the Great, Napoleon, the Bible's Queen Esther, Pocahontas, and George Washington, for example. Other spirits visualized by instruments belonged to pagans (those outside of Judeo-Christian religious traditions) from around the world: Africans, Eskimos, Asians, and Native Americans, seeking their eternal salvation through the Shakers. Events would, indeed, have seemed very strange to outsiders: Shakers acting "drunk" on spiritual "wine" or receiving as a group the "gift" of laughing until all were rolling on the floor. There was no telling who would become an instrument, giving voice to the spirit of someone who had died or going into a trance that could last for days. Some spiritual messages were for all Shakers, while some were advice or warnings targeted to individuals.

By the spring of 1838, Mother's Work had spread to Kentucky's South Union village; Elder Freegift Wells sent encouragement to Union Village that summer to be open to "gifts," and soon the Ohio Shakers were taking their share of spiritual journeys. They claimed to hear sounds from heaven, and one young boy spent a day and a half in a trance. A letter to North Union, Ohio, telling all about

Union Village's experiences had those Shakers experiencing Mother's Work as well. As the months went by, the spiritual gifts only increased throughout the sect. There were many new songs (often in unknown languages), dances, and marches being demonstrated. The "messages" that were critical of certain Shakers began to grow controversial. In fact, the elders began to require that messages be announced to them first, to determine if they were legitimate or from false spirits. Many devout Shakers doubted the authenticity of the spiritual phenomena, while some, like Philemon Stewart at New Lebanon, became full-time visionists or instruments.

The most welcome spirit was Holy Mother Wisdom, who Mother Ann had taught was the female part of God and who spoke through Sister Miranda Barber at New Lebanon in 1841. Believers prepared for her visits with fasting and footwashing. And though the Shakers did not allow pictures to decorate their buildings, inspired drawings became common. Sister Hannah Cahoon drew what she said Mother Ann called the "tree of life" and which became a favorite emblem of the Shaker faith. It was a tree "bearing ripe fruit" that "grows in the spirit land."[3] And a favorite hymn among the Shakers came about during this era to an elder at Alfred, Maine, called "Simple Gifts":

> 'Tis a gift to be simple, 'tis a gift to be free,
> 'Tis a gift to come down where we ought to be,
> And when we find ourselves in the place just right,
> We'll be in the valley of love and delight.

So certain were the Shakers that this was divine inspiration that they published a book version of it, Philemon Stewart's *A Holy,*

71

The Shakers went through a controversial era of spiritual renewal during a period they called "Mother's Work," which began in 1837. The "Tree of Life" is considered an inspired drawing done by a Shaker sister during that time.

Sacred and Divine Roll and Book, which he said was dictated to him by an angel. The book, a collection of quotations and religious reflections, warns that those who disobey its messages will be punished by God, and copies of the book were sent to world leaders. Stewart filled it with messages from Ann Lee and the biblical prophets, and called it sacred, but many of those who received it considered it more the devil's work. Within ten years, the Shakers took it out of circulation, and eventually Stewart lost the prominent position he held within the sect.

By about 1850, the exuberance of the visionary years had died down, and fewer messages were received by instruments; it wasn't ended by any one event, but it lost its momentum. Shakers such as Elder James Pote of Alfred, Maine, were glad to see it end, never fully believing that Mother's Work was actually the work of divine spirits. Historian Stephen Stein concluded that the era was actually harmful to the sect. "The religious commotion of the revival period threatened the stability of the United Society," he wrote, and led to pride more often than to true spiritual renewal. In fact, some of those who had been considered important instruments apostatized. It felt "awful beyond description" when two instruments left the New Lebanon Shakers in 1846 along with six other youths, wrote Elder Rufus Bishop.[4] Even Shaker leaders of the era came to believe that false spirits had often been mistaken for divine ones, and that too much time and energy had gone into devoting attention to all the events of the era.

Shakers reopened their worship services to the public, who eagerly returned for what they considered entertainment. But in general, these were the golden years for the United Society of

Believers, whose numbers had swelled to six thousand. Mother's Work had reinforced the important role of Mother Ann and other past leaders in Shaker doctrine and everyday life. Though the religious climate would change in America following the wrenching War Between the States in the 1860s, for now, there still were many Americans seeking the kind of salvation the Shakers promised.

FEWER MEMBERS, BUT STRONGER 7

*A*s the bloody Civil War wreaked its turmoil on the United States, the United Society of Believers had its own, less bloody battles to contend with, as elders and eldresses tried to keep Shaker members from deserting their "Heaven on Earth." One of the villages sent U.S. President Abraham Lincoln a Shaker rocking chair, perhaps in appreciation for his help in allowing Shakers to be exempt from military service during the war, and they received a thank-you note from Lincoln in 1864. From New Lebanon, family elders Frederick Evans and Benjamin Gates wrote Lincoln in late winter of 1865, expressing concern about his health and inviting him for a restful visit to New Lebanon. The Shakers, Lincoln was told in the letter, would "meet and receive you as sympathizing friends" who would "ask for no favors," but within a few weeks, Lincoln was dead.[1]

Apart from not contributing soldiers to the war effort, and their celibate life, the Shakers began to look and live more and more like

Eldresses Gertrude Soule and Bertha Lindsay walk through the village roads in Canterbury in this 1978 photograph.

the rest of America. Though told by their spiritual "visitors" back during Mother's Work to repent of their increasingly worldly ways, they instead went in just the opposite direction. Their once-plain clothing and buildings became more ornamental, while family elders and eldresses complained about an increasing lack of spirituality among the Believers. Rules were relaxed for fear that even more members would leave and join their former Shaker friends in the world. Wallpaper, carpet, and mirrors, once forbidden, began appearing in rooms, and gifts of jewelry and cologne weren't uncommon between members. "Vacations" were taken at beaches or Niagara Falls. The strict rules about men and women having little contact with each other were often ignored.

In smaller Shaker communities, such as Sabbathday Lake, Maine, elderly men and boys together had to do the work once done by young men. The membership figures had a negative impact on leadership, since the number of elders and eldresses needed was the same, but the number of good candidates from which to choose them only decreased, especially among men.

The Shaker population had peaked in the 1840s, with more than 3,600 members who had signed covenants; it began to dwindle steadily after that. Many of the new "members" were children, whom the Shakers had taken in with the hope they would grow into faithful Believers, since adult converts were becoming harder to come by. Parents often indentured their children to Shakers, or hired them out in exchange for the children's room and board. But all too often, the parents broke the contracts, and children who might have grown into Shakers were removed from the villages. In New Lebanon, for example, a man named William Pillow indentured his three sons to the village; the boys were happy, and their mother even joined one of the families there. But within a few months, Pillow came back to reclaim his family, none of whom wanted to leave, and Pillow left after an outburst of shouting and cursing. The next time he returned, he had a sheriff with him, and the boys were forced to leave.

There was a similar incident in Hancock at about the same time: a father accompanied by a sheriff dragged his two indentured daughters, ages nine and thirteen, away from the village as they cried and screamed, a heartbreaking experience for the Shakers looking on. The New Lebanon Shakers fought in court for three and a half years for the Pillow boys' return, but lost, as they often did. Even in the cases of broken contracts, judges usually sympathized with natural parents against the Shakers. There were many such legal battles, which became a large expense.

There were some conservative Shakers who called for a return to a more isolated Shaker life, as it had been generations earlier. In the east, Philemon Stewart gave elders what he claimed was an inspired piece of writing—a warning from God about the current Shakers' "Physical Sins"; he was told to keep his inspirations to himself.[2] Among western Believers, Hervey Eads, an elder and a Shaker since birth, was trying to woo Shakers back to their less worldly ways, which now included souvenir shops in the villages. But the conservative Shakers were literally dying out, and by the 1860s, more and more members were drawn to the progressive ideas put forth by leaders such as Frederick Evans and Antoinette Doolittle.

Doolittle had joined the Shakers at age fourteen against her parents' wishes. She became a forceful spokeswoman not just for other Shaker women but for women everywhere. She threw her support into the increasingly outspoken women's rights movement and became a prominent speaker and writer. Frederick Evans no doubt had one of the more unusual conversion stories among the Shakers. He had been active in reform movements in England, pushing for land reforms, better wages, and women's rights. He and his brother emigrated to the United States, and in New York they published a newspaper that called for an end to slavery and debtor prisons, equality for women, and even Sunday mail delivery. He was first a convert to socialism, the political and economic movement advocating people living together as equals and sharing resources. Evans therefore admired the lifestyle of the Shakers but thought they were "ignorant and fanatical."[3] Then he claimed to have been visited by angels, which convinced him to join the Believers. Articulate and passionate about his beliefs, Evans became the most well known Shaker of his time; he traveled, lectured, and made trips to England and Sweden to look for converts, though with little success. He became elder of New Lebanon's North Family, and though he never became an elder with the lead ministry, he was as influential as one. It was he, for example, who visited Abraham Lincoln in 1863 to discuss the Shakers' unwillingness to fight in any war.

With the blessings of leaders such as Evans, the Shakers began exploring other faiths and forms of spirituality. When the era of Mother's Work had ended around 1850, the "spirits" that had been such common visitors to Shaker villages spread elsewhere with the movement known as Spiritualism. Frederick Evans was among the visitors to the Rochester, New York, home where the two Fox sisters, Kate and Margaret, claimed to hear the rapping of spirits in the walls of their homes. Though it later proved to be a hoax, the notion of contacting spirits from other worlds took off in America, and many Shakers were equally enthusiastic about it. Like other

Americans, Shakers could be found holding seances to communicate with spirits. And rather than be concerned about the turn their religion was taking, elders and eldresses of the time expressed their pleasure at the interest younger Believers were taking in spiritual matters.

Nevertheless, the apostasies continued, usually over the issue of celibacy. Perhaps people also left because the Believers were losing the strong identity they once had and no longer stood apart from the world. The age of industrialization and progress brought more and more people to cities, and as the United States grew, rural populations everywhere began declining. Once popular Shaker products, such as their brooms, lost some of their value among the public because factories could mass-produce the same things for less money. But public interest in the Shakers themselves continued, at least for a while. One group of apostates, in fact, made their living traveling from town to town and acting out Shaker dances.

By 1870, the lead ministry had Shakers everywhere meeting for prayer services on Sunday evenings to pray for the sect. All were encouraged to spread the gospel and attract new members, perhaps among visitors or the hired hands at the villages. Fifty Shakers traveled to Boston and marched in Shaker fashion from their hotel to their meeting place. They sang hymns and had one of their union

Brother Frederick Evans never served as lead elder of the Shakers, but he acted as an official spokesman for them in the last half of the nineteenth century. He was considered "progressive" for his attempts to educate the Shakers and "the world's people" about each other.

Shakers had much success marketing their products, such as brooms, in the nineteenth century, until factories came along that could mass-produce items and charge less for them. But today, those handmade Shaker products, such as these wooden boxes, are highly valued.

meetings for the public, and Frederick Evans answered questions from the audience.

A monthly newspaper, *The Shaker*, was begun in 1871. It quoted a favorite Shaker verse from the Bible's Book of Haggai on its masthead: "I will shake all nations, and the desire of all nations shall come; and I will fill this house with glory, saith the Lord." Not only did the newspaper give Shakers a familiar voice to read, but it also attempted to explain to non-Shakers how the group tried to live an "angelic life," through celibacy, peace, and communal living. Celibacy was defended in the paper by a Watervliet writer: "Marriage peoples the earth but celibacy increases the forces of heaven," and the celibate life of Jesus was also pointed out.[4] The newspaper was quite liberal in its tone: one 1872 article carried the headline "Jesus a Sinner."[5] It reached a circulation peak of several thousand (there were many non-Shaker readers) and changed names three times before it finally folded in 1899. For a while Evans edited it and used it to promote causes such as equality between men and women, the advantages of a vegetarian diet, and the social problems caused by air and water pollution.

In 1874, a journalist named Charles Nordhoff spent much time with the Shakers while he researched his book, *Communistic Societies of the United States*. He concluded that of the various groups that had tried communal living in the United States, the Shakers had been most successful. He believed they were too preoccupied with neatness and cleanliness, but at the same time found them to be pleasant. He also noted the diversity among their members. For example, some families followed strict vegetarian diets, while Kentucky Shakers preferred rich southern foods. Nordhoff's census count of the United Society of Believers was 1,189 women, 695 men, 339 girls, and 192 boys: just over 2,400 Shaker residents total, living on or owners of almost 100,000 acres (40,500 ha) of land.

South Union, Kentucky, and the villages in the east included African-American residents. In Philadelphia, a black woman named

Rebecca Jackson led a household of African-Americans who lived a Shaker life in the city. Jackson first lived in Watervliet, then left to preach the Shaker gospel, to whomever would listen, in Philadelphia. The Shakers had hoped more urban Shaker centers like Jackson's would come about; like more converts in general, however, none ever materialized.

The first real acknowledgment of the Shakers' decline came in the mid-1870s, when the village at Tyringham, Massachusetts, was closed, its property sold off, and its residents moved to Enfield, Connecticut. Charles Nordhoff had counted only seventeen residents at Tyringham in 1874. In just ten years, from 1860 to 1870, the population of the eastern communities shrank by one-third. As village closings continued, the Shakers, led by progressives like Evans and Doolittle, threw their energy into helping the reform movements sweeping the country. Shaker leaders seemed finally to accept that gathering in new members, as promised by various spiritual visitors during Mother's Work, wasn't likely to happen, and so their attention turned increasingly outward, even as remaining Shakers tried not to lose heart. "Our number is small but the feeling is strong," read one entry in Watervliet's Second Family's journal in 1885.[6] Once forbidden to read anything not approved by leadership, Believers now were encouraged to read more about the world and to discuss current social topics in their union meetings.

Membership figures would decline another 50 percent by the year 1900, and many of those remaining were elderly. In New Lebanon's Church Family, *none* of the 110 children taken in between 1871 and 1900 became adult Shakers. The younger, more worldly Believers began to lose sight of Shaker traditions; men began growing beards (they had customarily been clean-shaven), and musical instruments such as organs accompanied the always smaller number of voices singing. One older sister wrote of trying to teach a group of young Shakers some of the songs and dances she remembered from years gone by. She had to give it up because her "students" were laughing too hard! But one Shaker tradition that was maintained was the celebration of Mother Ann's birthday each winter.

It would have been easy for Shakers in the late 1800s to dwell on bad news. Because of declining numbers, the quality of leadership became more and more of an issue. John Cumings was a lifelong Shaker living in Enfield, Connecticut, whose letters to his non-Shaker family members in the 1870s illustrate the frustration felt by many Believers in that transitional era. In one letter, he confessed to believing little of the doctrine anymore but also felt he could not leave. In another letter, to his sister, he complained about five elders leaving his Shaker family since he had signed the covenant. Sometimes downright bad leaders remained in their positions because there was nobody to replace them. Then, as the population aged, senility became a problem among elders. Temporal and spiritual leadership positions, such as those of elder, deacon, and trustee, often had to be combined.

Even when bad leaders left the Society, the problems they caused could remain long after. One man who apostatized from the New Lebanon East Family left a $20,000 debt behind. Trustees, who by themselves oversaw sometimes very large sums of money during more prosperous times, could be especially damaging. One elder, Thomas Damon of Hancock, estimated in the 1870s that over a fifty-year period, the Believers lost more than $200,000 because of apostasy and money mismanagement on the part of trustees. Damon suggested that more women be allowed to be trustees; as the male ranks thinned out, this became a necessity.

By the 1880s, due to their increasing average age, the Believers ceased their dancing during worship, ending a hundred-year tradition. Their services became simpler, with Scripture readings, hymn

Men and women got together each week for "Union Meetings," where they had a chance to visit and form "helpful" friendships—a man might need help mending clothes, for example, while women might need to have wood chopped for their kitchen stoves.

singing, and public "testimonies" by members. The public had finally grown uninterested in Shaker worship services, and few outsiders filed in through the visitors' doors on Sundays. In 1889, another village closed, in North Union, Ohio. Once two hundred members strong, it had less than one-fourth that number by 1880.

The western villages had an especially hard time as membership declined. Perhaps because they remained long-distance "relatives" of the eastern Shakers, the leadership problems remained more severe among the western Shakers. North Union's last years were a struggle of renting out land, hiring laborers for its broom business, and selling rock from a quarry on its property in order to keep the village going. All of the Shaker villages were saddled with much work just to maintain the now-unnecessary buildings erected during earlier, more prosperous years. The Shakers of North Union moved south to Union Village; the next closing came in 1892 at Groveland, New York, whose residents moved to Watervliet. Being forced to move could be traumatic, especially for the elderly Shakers. When the village at Watervliet closed its Second Family dwelling, its sixty-five-year-old eldress refused to leave it; she was allowed to remain there until her death in 1913, though it meant expenses to heat and maintain it.

Over the next several decades, the Society of Believers would busy themselves with disposing of property, buildings, and livestock and readjusting to what slowly became a single-sex church. After serving as a family elder and unofficial Shaker spokesman, Frederick Evans died in 1893 at age eighty-five, and women Shakers gradually enjoyed more visibility as leaders and writers. Antoinette Doolittle became an able lecturer and writer, and in 1904, two other eldresses from Mount Lebanon, New York, Anna White and Leila S. Taylor, published a four-hundred-page book, *Shakerism: Its Meaning and Message*, which expressed confidence that someday people would rediscover the value of the Society of Believers. Catherine Allen, appointed to the head ministry in 1908, helped lead a petition drive for women's suffrage. But most Shaker women were busier than ever with their domestic duties, made more burdensome as the women aged. One Watervliet sister wrote in a journal that sisters there were "working every minute getting ready for the Christmas sale" and were "almost killing themselves." Shaker women earned important incomes with their crafts, such as boxes, baskets, fans, dolls, and specialty foods. Each village had a shop for visitors, and traveling salespeople peddled the crafts, too.

The Shakers made one last attempt at growth at the end of the 1800s when they bought almost 60,000 acres (24,000 ha) of land in Georgia and more than 7,000 acres (2,830 ha) in Florida. In Georgia, converts never came, and most of the residents were transplanted Shakers from Ohio. By 1902, they had their land up for sale. The story repeated itself in Florida, where New England Shakers thought they could grow pineapples as well as attract new members. But the "Olive Branch" community established there never had more than a dozen members, and it was dissolved in 1911.

The main source of income for the Believers by then was selling off land and assets. For example, the state of Massachusetts bought the Shakers' land at Shirley for $43,000 in 1908, and Whitewater land in Ohio was sold in 1910 for $40,000. Like other Americans, the now worldly Shakers became interested in investing their money in new technology. As they sold off property, the trustees had large amounts to wheel and deal with—not always

Many of the old Shaker villages have been turned into museums, where visitors can see how the Shakers lived and flourished in the nineteenth century.

successfully. An early example occurred at Union Village, where a trustee invested $16,000 in a Dayton, Ohio, company making a new type of furnace, which, unfortunately, didn't make any money. The financial loss was made worse by a fire and a tornado, causing more hardship for the village. That sort of bad judgment by a trustee caused a loss of members, too, as Elder Giles Avery noted. In tough times, the villages helped each other out, as they also helped their non-Shaker neighbors and other causes. And as women began to assume the family trustee positions there were fewer incidents of loss, as they seemed less inclined to risk large sums of money.

But life wasn't always so harsh. As rules relaxed, more Shakers enjoyed life's small pleasures, such as playing games of checkers, dominoes, or croquet; they fished, went on sleigh rides or berry-picking expeditions, and visited resorts or other Shaker friends. Christmas had once been reserved as a day of confession, a habit established by Father Joseph Meacham. Now they had festive Christmas holidays, with singing, Christmas trees, and gift exchanges. They attended lectures and civic meetings, like those of the Women's Christian Temperance Union; in 1905 the Shakers at New Lebanon organized a peace conference. In fact, worship services became more infrequent as recreation seemed to become more common. Those who remained in the Society of Believers were hardly the isolated Shakers of a hundred years earlier: not only did the Shakers eagerly embrace the new telephone in the 1880s, they invested in it, too. Use of electric lights instead of candles and steam heat instead of wood stoves led to a big decrease in fires among the villages. As the twentieth century progressed, Shakers loved to pose for photographs with another favorite modern convenience—the automobile.

Much as they isolated themselves in their villages, the Shakers almost always embraced new technology, such as the automobile at the turn of the twentieth century.

In the year 1900, there were 885 Shakers, almost one-third of them age sixty or older. Sister Genevieve DeGraw wrote a verse about the realities of Shaker life:

One by one they're passing on,
Friends we long have known;
But we'll meet them all again
In our spirit home.[7]

CARRYING ON

8

By the 1940s, all of the Shaker villages were governed by elderly sisters. Sabbathday Lake Eldress Prudence Stickney, age seventy-one, wrote to another eldress, "I think of all the few remaining brave souls, and talk to our dear departed saints about it, but the answers never come back."[1] In 1947, New Lebanon, now known as Mount Lebanon, closed, its sisters moving to Hancock, Massachusetts. The Great Depression of the 1930s hastened the difficult situation of the sect, and Canterbury in New Hampshire and Sabbathday Lake were the only other remaining Shaker villages. For some of the elderly women, moving to a new home when theirs shut down was devastating.

The last men serving as lead elders died in the 1930s. There were forty Shakers left in the early 1950s, two of whom were brothers. Ten years later, Hancock was closed, and the brothers had died. Most of the Shaker women were resigned to imagining a world without Shakers; the healthier ones spent much time taking care of the weaker sisters. Church services were seldom held and were more likely to be watched on television.

Lead eldress Emma B. King, who lived at Canterbury, publicly declared that decline did not equal failure. In the meantime, she set up the Shaker Central Trust Fund, run by three Believers and three lawyers. Money from property and asset sales went into that and helped support the remaining Shakers. By 1965, Eldress King, age ninety-one, decided it was time to close the Society to new members.

Ironically, she did that at a time when genuine interest in the Society, fueled by the Shaker antique craze, was showing a few sprouts in what had appeared to be a barren field. Shaker historian Stephen Stein made note of the differences between the Shakers at Canterbury and those at Sabbathday Lake. United in Shaker gospel for nearly two centuries, the two communities took very different viewpoints on what appeared to be the end of those who maintained that gospel. Emma King and the other women at Canterbury were resigned to doing their jobs and being the last Shakers; they

Emma B. King was the last official lead eldress of the Shakers, and, at age ninety, was still leading the sect in the 1960s. A division occurred between the remaining two villages, Canterbury and Sabbathday Lake, when Emma King at Canterbury closed the Shakers to any new members, while Sabbathday Lake admitted a new member, Theodore Johnson. Brother Ted was never recognized by the sisters at Canterbury as a true Shaker.

may have been fearful that some might be attracted to the trust fund more than to the gospel. At Sabbathday Lake, getting by financially had always been more of a struggle in the harsher terrain, and so perhaps they had learned that their strong faith and optimism had its just rewards. They were more receptive and trusting of the young people who were curious about them.

Ted Johnson was the first man to join the Shakers in decades. After him, two more young male members, Arnold Hadd and Wayne Smith, joined the Shakers in Sabbathday Lake and remain there today.

In any case, a friend and helper to the Sabbathday Lake Shakers, Theodore Johnson, wanted to join the Society as a brother, and the sisters in Maine were eager to accept him. A former Sabbathday Lake eldress who switched her alliances and moved to Canterbury told a newspaper reporter that Johnson should not be admitted because there were no male members who could teach him. The Sabbathday sisters disagreed with that reasoning, and they admitted him, calling him Brother Ted. In fact, Johnson believed that many of the young visitors to the Maine community might have joined if it hadn't been for the 1965 membership "cutoff." Though not recognized as an authentic Shaker by the Canterbury sisters, Brother Ted was considered a vital part of the Sabbathday Lake community and was much loved by his "sisters" there.

Thirty years ago those Shakers still living were considered the "last" Shakers, but that isn't so easily assumed anymore. Although Brother Ted died unexpectedly in 1986, and the community at Canterbury closed in 1992, today Sabbathday Lake is joined by two other young male converts; the eight community members there are headed by Frances Carr, the last member to officially sign a covenant, and members now range in age from their thirties to their eighties.

They carry on Shaker life as they work in the large herb garden or tend the sheep; they gather together for meals cooked by Frances Carr. After breakfast, the group reads from the Bible and prays for Shakers, living or passed away, as well as other special intentions and concerns about the world. Groups and individuals come to study and pray with them, and each week a meal is prepared for and shared with a shelter for homeless people. Frances Carr doesn't believe that they will be the "last" Shakers.

The Sabbathday Lake Shakers today are under the leadership of Frances Carr, shown here, and Arnold Hadd.

A hundred years ago, a Shaker sister saw her church in decline but made a poetic prediction that seems to have come to pass:

> *Though Zion's numbers may be reduced. . . , yet there will always be a few, who will take the work of God as it is, & feel that His yoke is easy, & His burden is light.*[2]

Brother Ted Johnson and brother Arnold Hadd; Johnson died in 1986.

The Sabbathday Lake Shaker village today

SOURCE NOTES

Chapter 2

1. Edward R. Horgan, *The Shaker Holy Land: A Community Portrait* (Harvard, Mass.: Harvard Common Press, 1982), p. 12.
2. Stephen J. Stein, *The Shaker Experience in America* (New Haven, Conn.: Yale University Press, 1992), p. 11.
3. Priscilla J. Brewer, *Shaker Communities, Shaker Lives* (Hanover, N.H.: University Press of New England, 1986), p. 5.
4. Horgan, p. 16.
5. Horgan, p. 25.
6. Ibid.
7. Ibid.

Chapter 3

1. Stephen J. Stein, *The Shaker Experience in America* (New Haven, Conn.: Yale University Press, 1992), pp. 35–36.
2. Flo Morse, *The Story of the Shakers* (Woodstock, Vt.: Countryman Press, 1986), p. 17.

3. Stein, p. 36.

4. Priscilla J. Brewer, *Shaker Communities, Shaker Lives* (Hanover, N.H.: University Press of New England, 1986), p. 17.

5. Morse, p. 19.

6. Brewer, p. 23.

Chapter 4

1. Stephen J. Stein, *The Shaker Experience in America* (New Haven, Conn.: Yale University Press, 1992), p. 49.

2. Thomas Brown, *An Account of the People Called Shakers* (Troy, N.Y.: Parker and Bliss, 1812), p. 22.

3. Priscilla J. Brewer, *Shaker Communities, Shaker Lives* (Hanover, N.H.: University Press of New England, 1986), p. 33.

4. Stein, p. 61.

5. Brewer, p. 34.

6. Flo Morse, *The Story of the Shakers* (Woodstock, Vt.: Countryman Press, 1986), p. 28.

7. Brewer, p. 36.

8. Ibid.

9. Stein, p. 107.

Chapter 5

1. Stephen J. Stein, *The Shaker Experience in America* (New Haven, Conn.: Yale University Press, 1992), p. 103.

2. Priscilla J. Brewer, *Shaker Communities, Shaker Lives* (Hanover, N.H.: University Press of New England, 1986), p. 53.

3. Brewer, p. 66.

4. Brewer, p. 68.

5. Brewer, p. 75.

6. Brewer, p. 77.

Chapter 6

1. Stephen J. Stein, *The Shaker Experience in America* (New Haven, Conn.: Yale University Press, 1992), p. 163.
2. Flo Morse, *The Story of the Shakers* (Woodstock, Vt.: Countryman Press, 1986), pp. 33–34.
3. Morse, p. 41.
4. Stein, p. 184.

Chapter 7

1. Stephen J. Stein, *The Shaker Experience in America* (New Haven, Conn.: Yale University Press, 1992), p. 203.
2. Stein, p. 205.
3. Stein, p. 206.
4. Stein, p. 226.
5. Priscilla J. Brewer, *Shaker Communities, Shaker Lives* (Hanover, N.H.: University Press of New England, 1986), p. 194.
6. Stein, p. 242.
7. Stein, p. 341.

Chapter 8

1. Stephen J. Stein, *The Shaker Experience in America* (New Haven, Conn.: Yale University Press, 1992), p. 350.
2. Stein, p. 250.

FOR FURTHER READING

Brewer, Priscilla J. *Shaker Communities, Shaker Lives.* Hanover, N.H.: University Press of New England, 1986.

Carr, Sister Frances A. *Growing Up Shaker.* Sabbathday Lake, Maine: The United Society of Shakers, 1994.

Horgan, Edward R. *The Shaker Holy Land: A Community Portrait.* Harvard, Mass.: Harvard Common Press, 1982.

Morse, Flo. *The Story of the Shakers.* Woodstock, Vt.: Countryman Press, 1986.

Stein, Stephen J. *The Shaker Experience in America: A History of the United Society of Believers.* New Haven, Conn.: Yale University Press, 1992.

INTERNET SITES

Due to the changeable nature of the Internet, sites appear and disappear very quickly. Internet addresses must be entered with capital and lowercase letters exactly as they appear.

The Yahoo directory of the World Wide Web is an excellent place to find Internet sites on any topic. The directory is located at:

http://www.yahoo.com

The Shaker Village at Canterbury, New Hampshire, is now a museum that preserves and interprets Shaker history and ideals. The village maintains a Web site that includes songs, recipes, and a village tour:

http://newww.com/org/csv/

The Shaker Village at Hancock, Massachusetts, is also an outdoor museum with its own Web site, with pages about buildings, farming, crafts, and other activities at the village:

http://www.hancockshakervillage.org/

INDEX

ABOUT THE AUTHOR

Jean Kinney Williams grew up in Ohio and lives there now with her husband and four children. She studied journalism in college and, in addition to writing, enjoys reading, volunteering at church, and spending time with her family. She is the author of the Franklin Watts First Book *Matthew Hensen: Polar Adventurer* (1994) and of three other American Religious Experience books, *The Amish* (1996), *The Christian Scientists* (1997), and *The Mormons* (1996).

MONROE CO. LIB

3 5001 42188901 2

J 289. 80973 William
Williams, Jean Kinney.
The Shakers

0531113426 (lib. bdg.)
BD   7-98

Monroe County Library System
Monroe, Michigan 48161